Ten Common
Home Decorating Mistakes
& How to Avoid Them

Gloria Hander Lyons

Blue Sage Press

Ten Common Home Decorating Mistakes
& How to Avoid Them

Inquires should be addressed to:
Blue Sage Press
48 Borondo Pines
La Marque, TX 77568
www.BlueSagePress.com

ISBN-13: 978-0-9802244-4-3

Library of Congress Control Number: 2008910163

First Edition: November 2008

Printed in the United States of America

Table of Contents

More Decorating Ideas

Introduction

Ten Common Home Decorating Mistakes & How to Avoid Them

Our homes should be a comfortable retreat—an escape from the hectic world outside. When you step inside your home, you should feel the immediate sense of relief and joy that having a comfortable, attractive living space can provide. But there are several common decorating mistakes that might be causing trouble.

If you feel that your rooms aren't quite "working" for you, but you're not sure why, keep reading. You might just find the answers to your decorating dilemmas in the next few chapters.

This book offers helpful hints and creative ideas for furniture layouts, color schemes, lighting, window treatments, accessorizing and more that can help you achieve the results you want.

There's no need to toss out all your furniture and start over to create a more inviting space. These decorating suggestions are helpful whether you're starting from scratch with an empty room or planning to use what you already own.

Decorating your home should be fun and rewarding. Your goal should always be to create a space that makes you happy, based on your own personal style—not popular trends or someone else's opinions. So surround yourself with items you love—things that will add joy to your life each time you see them.

Apply these helpful tips to make the most efficient use of your space, choose the right furniture pieces and lighting to make your rooms function better, and create an inviting mood to make the time you spend there more enjoyable.

Whether you plan to start with an empty space or decorate using the furniture and accessories you already own, this simple step-by-step guide can help make your rooms more functional, as well as more attractive, using whatever budget you choose.

Mistake #1:
A Room
Without a
Cause

Many times a room isn't "working" for us because we simply haven't thought about how we need it to function; therefore, the room doesn't have the appropriate furniture or lighting to meet our needs.

Do you long for a comfortable chair with sufficient light in your bedroom for reading? Do you desperately need more seating in your living room to accommodate guests? Where could you possibly squeeze in a desk for computer work? Don't live with the frustration of doing without—fix the problem. Before starting any new decorating project, take the time to decide how you need the space to function.

This task isn't complicated. It just takes some thought. If you plan to redecorate your living room, take a few moments to decide what activities you'll be doing in the space. Will you be watching television? Do you need a comfortable conversation area for entertaining? How many people will you need to accommodate for seating?

Would you also like to have a comfortable reading area separate from the main seating group? Do you have enough space to include a game table or writing desk in the room, as well? Creating rooms with multiple functions is a great way to make more efficient use of your space.

Follow this same process for designing a dining room. Think about your entertainment needs for parties, dinner guests and holiday events. How many people are involved? Is the event usually formal or casual? How often do you hold each type of gathering?

For your bedrooms, consider how many people you need to accommodate in each room. Do your kids need a desk for homework or do they need more storage for toys? Do you want to use one of your bedrooms for a home office? Would the office also need to function as a guest bedroom?

Taking the time to consider the functional needs for your design project will help you decide what furniture pieces and lighting you'll need. Make a list of these items. Then, simply remove any pieces of furniture that don't meet your functional needs and replace them with ones that work.

Are you planning to do an interior re-design, where you'll be using the furniture and accessories you already own, or do you plan to purchase all new pieces or just a few new items? If you're doing an interior re-design, scour your entire house to find furniture and lighting that will help make your room more functional. If you want to add new furniture, you'll have a list of the pieces you need to buy.

Most of us have limited space in our homes, so it's important to use the space we have efficiently. Don't just "make do" with the current condition of your living areas. Take the time to figure out how you need your rooms to function and make them "work" for you!

Mistake #2: What's the Point?

Ignoring the focal point in a room is a very common decorating mistake. When planning your design project, make an effort to highlight an architectural feature in the room or create an attractive vignette on one of the walls, which can serve as the room's focal point. It will make the time you spend there more enjoyable, and that is, after all, what decorating is about—adding more beauty to our lives.

The focal point can be a fireplace with attractive decorations above the mantel, a window with a beautiful view, artwork arranged over a sofa, or even an entertainment center, if the main function of the room is watching television instead conversation.

If you have a room with a nice view, make it the focal point of your room. Arrange the furniture to draw attention toward it. Frame the window with drapery panels or fabric swags and position a tall plant or topiary on either side to help make it stand out, as shown at left.

If the fireplace is an attractive architectural feature in your living room, orient your furniture toward it. In the furniture layout below (Figure 1), the sofa is facing the fireplace, with two upholstered chairs across from it, creating a comfortable conversation area.

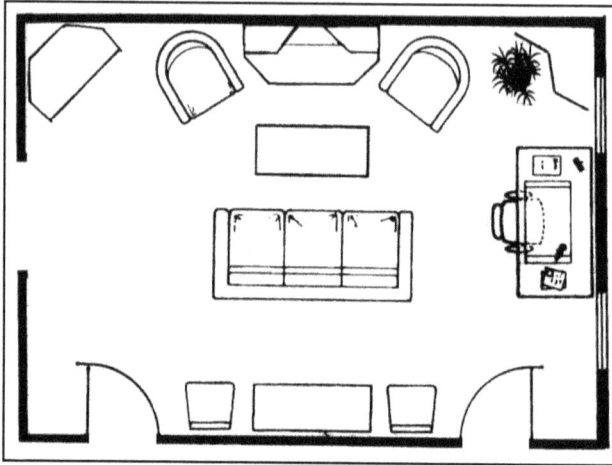

Figure 1

The focal point of any room should create sufficient impact to draw your attention. When using the fireplace as the focal point, arrange a group of accessories, such as framed mirrors, paintings, vases, candles and other objects on or over the mantle in order to create a pleasing composition and make your focal point stand out.

Try to make the composition large enough in scale and extended high enough on the wall above the mantel shelf to establish its importance. How do you know if your arrangement works? Just stand back and observe. Does the composition appear pleasing and relatively balanced? Does it create enough of an impact to draw your attention? As long as you're happy with the results and you've taken the time to check the overall impact, then go with it!

A good example for an arrangement above a fireplace mantle is a large painting hung above the mantel shelf, in the center, and two identical candlesticks or vases placed on either side of the painting as shown in Figure 2 below.

Figure 2   **Figure 3**

You don't need to use a perfectly symmetrical arrangement of accessories over your fireplace mantle (called "formal balance") as shown in Figure 2. This type of composition creates a formal, traditional look. You can also create a more casual arrangement (informal balance) from a group of objects of varying sizes and shapes. With this type of arrangement, you'll need to do some experimenting with different combinations of objects until you feel the balance looks right.

An example of informal balance is a large framed mirror placed on the mantel shelf, slightly off center, which is balanced by a vase filled with tall branches as shown in Figure 3.

7

Painting an accent wall in a darker or more vibrant color that contrasts with the fireplace or other objects in your focal point is another way to make it stand out. For example, if your fireplace has white wood trim and your room is painted a neutral beige color, then painting the wall that the fireplace is on with a darker shade of beige (or one of your accent colors in the room, such as medium blue) will draw the eye to that wall. It will also make the fireplace "pop" because of the white paint of the wood trim against the darker wall color. Placing any object in front of a sharply contrasting color makes it more visible.

If you don't have a fireplace in your living room, you can create a focal point by arranging decorative objects and artwork over a sofa or an attractive piece of furniture, such as a chest or entry table. Painting an accent wall in a contrasting color behind these arrangements will also create more impact for your focal point.

Focal points should not be reserved for just the living room. Whether it's an arrangement of plates over a buffet in your dining room or an attractive curtain panel behind the headboard of your bed, have fun experimenting with arrangements in other rooms in your home, to create attractive vignettes you can enjoy throughout your house.

Mistake #3: "I Can't Hear You!"

Many homeowners tend to place all the furniture in the living room up against the walls, leaving a huge empty space in the middle of the room, which creates an awkward conversation area.

The seating arrangement for the living room needs to be close enough to carry on a comfortable conversation without having to yell at someone on the other side of the room. See Figure 1 below.

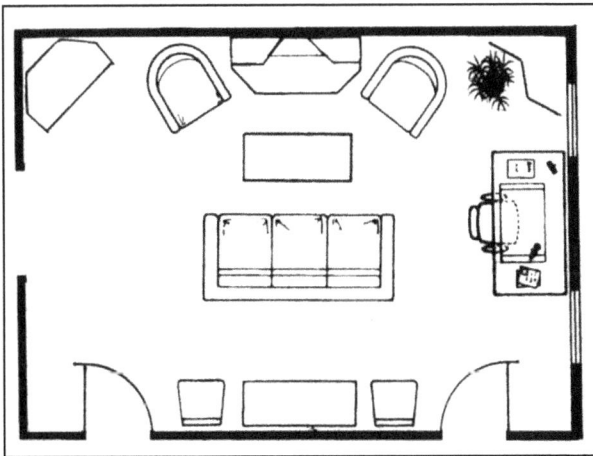

Figure 1

The furniture for a conversation group usually includes a sofa and two upholstered chairs, all facing each other, which makes it easier to see, as well as hear, the members of the group. It is also convenient to have a coffee table in the center of the conversation area, as shown in Figure 1, placed close enough so that guests can easily reach a beverage from the table without getting out of their seats.

The furniture list you made when you decided on the function of your room will tell you how much seating you will need. You might prefer to have four upholstered chairs facing each other instead of a sofa and two chairs.

If you need seating for six to eight people on a regular basis, you might need two sofas and two chairs. Whatever combination of seating you choose, try to group them in an arrangement that is comfortable for conversation.

By pulling your conversation-area furniture into a smaller, more functional group, you might be able to create space in the rest of the room for other activities (such as a game table, a separate reading area or writing desk) if space allows, as the designers have done in Figure 1. Creating rooms with multi-functions is a great way to make more efficient use of your space.

Arrange the furniture you need in your living room to create a comfortable conversation area. When you're finished, stand back and take note of the visual weight and size of the furniture placed throughout the room.

Do you have too many large (or visually heavy) pieces on one side of the room, making it feel out of balance? Do you have any empty corners that need to be addressed? If so, make a few adjustments and add objects as needed to try to make the room feel more balanced.

Look at Figure 1 on page 9. The designers placed a corner entertainment center and a writing desk in the room for additional activity areas, then added a standing screen and plant to fill in an empty corner.

Check your furniture layout for overall balance and add objects such as plants, screens, benches, small tables, etc. to any areas that might seem bare.

Furniture Arranging Tips:

A few furniture arranging tips are listed below that might be helpful when planning the furniture layout for your rooms.

1. Avoid lining all your furniture up against the walls, making your room feel like an office waiting area. Start by pulling your conversation area furniture into a tight group in the center of the room if space allows, as shown in Figure 1 on page 9.

2. Try placing your furniture on the diagonal instead of square with the walls. Arranging the conversation area diagonally in your room can add a sense of motion. Repeating this angle by placing other furniture pieces on the diagonal will create continuity. See the "before" layout in Figure A on page 12.

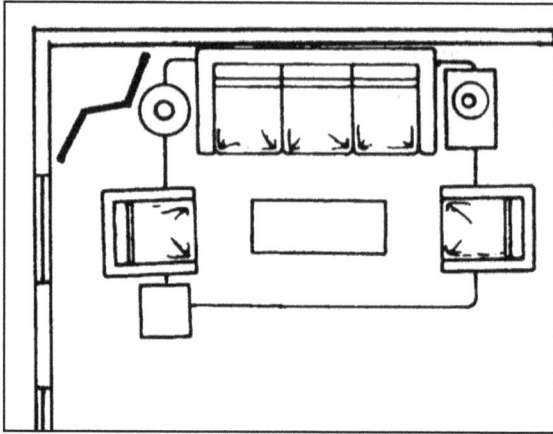

Figure A

In Figure A, the sofa and chairs are square with the walls. This arrangement is functional, but it gives the room a rather static feel. The sofa is flanked by an end table with a lamp on the right and a floor lamp on the left. A standing screen is placed in the corner.

In the "after" layout shown in Figure B on page 13, the sofa is placed on an angle in the corner in front of the standing screen and a sofa table for displaying accessories. This arrangement creates the focal point of the room, since the space has no prominent architectural feature.

The sofa is flanked by an end table on the right and a floor lamp on the left. The chairs, as well as the area rug, are also placed on an angle. The coffee table has been replaced by an ottoman which doubles as a coffee table.

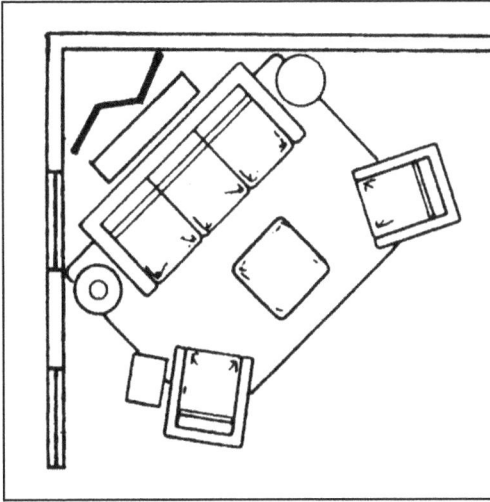

Figure B

3. Try to balance the number of wood and upholstered pieces you use in the room. Too many hard surfaces make the space feel cold and uninviting. Use fabrics, plants (real or silk), rugs, pillows, throws, etc. to add softness and warmth.

4. If you don't have room to include end tables for lighting next to your sofa, pull the sofa away from the wall just far enough to place a long, narrow sofa table behind it to hold lamps and interesting accessories. See the example in Figure B above.

5. If the room is a long, rectangular shape, divide it into two or three separate activity areas, such as reading, watching television, or sitting by the fire. See Figure C on page 14.

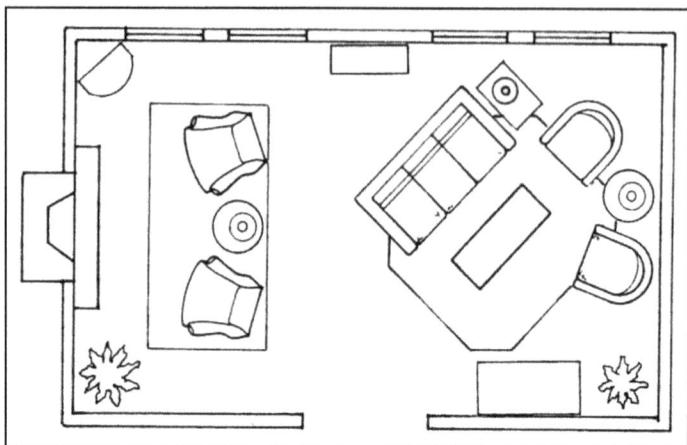

Figure C

In the furniture layout above, the designer has divided the long, rectangular room into two separate seating areas. On the left side of the room, two wing-back chairs were arranged in front of the fireplace for a relaxing place to read or enjoy the fire. A lamp was added to the table in between the two chairs for task lighting.

There is a comfortable conversation area on the right side of the room, placed on an angle to create a more welcoming approach from the room's entrance. An entertainment center was included in this area for watching television. Both seating groups were anchored with area rugs to help define the separate spaces.

Try rearranging the furniture in your living areas to create a more comfortable conversation area. Include the furniture that you need to make your space more functional. After creating your layout, check to see that the furniture is distributed evenly throughout the room.

14

Mistake #4:
Road Blocks

Does your current furniture layout make you feel like you're running through a maze of detours and road blocks? Blocking the flow of traffic is another common decorating problem that can cause a room to feel awkward.

Before creating a new furniture arrangement, take note of where the traffic patterns are in your room, so you'll remember to leave these areas free of furniture.

- Try to avoid placing any large pieces of furniture close to the entrance to the room, which might create a road block for traffic.

- Make sure there is enough room for people to walk through the space comfortably without bumping into furniture. Traffic paths should be about three feet wide if possible.

- Leave space for traffic to get from one side of the room to the other without cutting through the center of your conversation area. The ideal arrangement is to have the traffic flow around the perimeter of the room, if space allows.

Examples of living room furniture arrangements that might cause traffic flow problems are listed below:

1. Overcrowding your room with too much furniture. Solution: Refer to the furniture list you created when determining the function of the room. Remove any pieces of furniture that aren't absolutely necessary.

2. Using furniture that is too large for the space. Solution: Trade them out with smaller pieces in your home, purchase new ones that are more suitable in scale, or reduce the number of pieces in the room.

3. Pushing all the furniture up against the walls, forcing traffic through the conversation area, as shown in Figure D below.

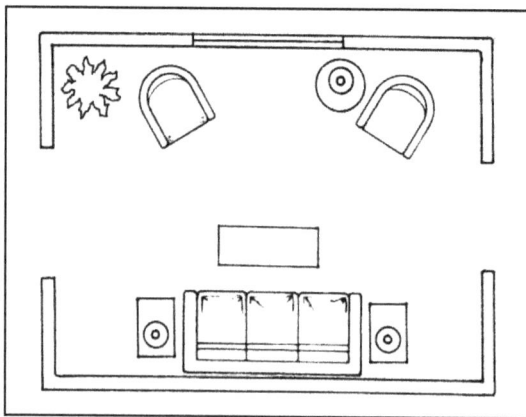

Figure D

Solution: If your living room is too small to pull the furniture off the walls into a smaller conversation area that allows traffic to flow around it, then anchor the sofa against the longest wall, with the chairs facing each other, perpendicular to the sofa, or opposite the sofa as shown in Figure E below. This will keep the conversation area together and allow traffic to flow around one side. The designer also used an area rug to help anchor the seating area.

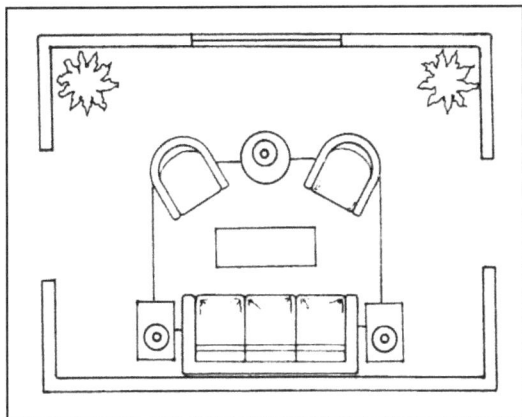

Figure E

4. A sofa or chair that blocks the main entrance to a room. Solution: Rotate your seating arrangement, moving the offending sofa or chair to one of the walls in the room. It's usually best to place the sofa against the longest wall if the room is not large enough to float the seating area somewhere in the room. Try to avoid blocking the entrance to your room with a large piece of furniture.

Look at the before and after furniture layouts on page 18, showing an example of blocking the entrance to a room. In Figure F, the sofa is blocking the room's only entrance. The furniture arrangement doesn't allow for easy access to the seating area.

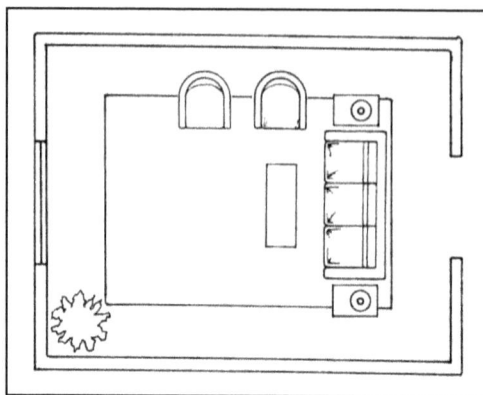

Figure F

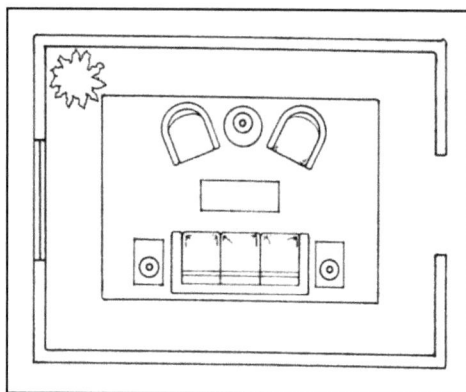

Figure G

Figure G shows how the furniture layout was rotated to open up the entrance, creating a more welcoming feel. The club chairs were also repositioned across from the sofa, to provide a more comfortable conversation area.

Pay careful attention to where the traffic patterns are in your room, and place your furniture to promote a comfortable flow. An inviting furniture layout should draw you into the space—not put up a road-block in your path. Arrange your furniture so that it welcomes you into the room.

Mistake #5:
Slightly Off-Kilter

Balance is a very important element when decorating a room. Whether referring to the placement of furniture, color or lighting, it's important to distribute them evenly throughout the space, or the room will feel off balance.

In addition to distributing the furniture evenly around the room, you should also check for balance in the height of the furniture pieces in the room. This doesn't mean that all the furniture pieces should be the same height. What you want is a mixture of heights—some tall objects and some low objects, to create an interesting mix.

After creating your furniture layout, simply check to see that the taller pieces are dispersed evenly around the room, otherwise, the room will feel out of balance.

If you have a tall piece of furniture on one wall, try to balance it on the opposite wall with another tall piece of furniture, or a lower piece of furniture with artwork arranged over it that will create enough visual weight on the wall to balance the taller piece of furniture.

Balance is important in creating harmony in your space. We have already discussed distributing your furniture evenly around the room when arranging your furniture.

We also discussed creating a focal point by displaying decorative items on your focal point wall in an attractive composition that appears balanced.

Use this same technique to achieve balance for all the wall elevations in your room. You can use either "formal balance", where the arrangement is perfectly symmetrical, using identical pieces of furniture, such as a chest of drawers in the center with matching chairs placed on either side. Or you can use "informal balance", using objects of different shapes and sizes, that you arrange into a composition that you feel is visually balanced.

An example of creating balance on a wall elevation is listed below:

1. Start by placing the largest piece of furniture in the center of the wall. In this example, we'll use a sofa.

2. Add the next most important pieces, such as end tables on each end of the sofa. Try to keep them about the same height if they are not identical.

3. Arrange accessories, such as lamps, placed on the end tables. They can be identical pieces or visually balanced pieces (lamps that are not identical, but are equal in visual weight).

4. Create a balanced display of artwork over the back of the sofa.

Look at Figure 4 on page 21.

Figure 4

Figure 4 shows an example of formal balance on a wall elevation. Each side of the arrangement is identical. The example below in Figure 5 shows informal balance, described on page 22.

Figure 5

In the informal balance example shown in Figure 5, the designer used a visually heavier table on the right side of the sofa than the one on the left. She then placed a visually heavier lamp on the left side to help create balance.

Since she felt the right side of the furniture arrangement still appeared heavier, she placed a large framed mirror on the wall on the left side of the wall art arrangement, then a visually lighter grouping of wall art on the right side to achieve overall balance in the wall elevation.

Creating a composition of furniture and accessories using informal balance takes a bit of experimenting until you feel the arrangement looks right. Just keep trying different combinations of objects until you are pleased with the overall look.

Visual Weight:

An example of comparing the visual weight of objects is two table lamps that are exactly the same height, but the base of one lamp is thin, like a turned wooden base, and the other has a fuller shape, like a Ginger jar. The lamp with the fuller-shaped base appears to have more visual weight than the thinner lamp base. Look at the example below.

The same idea applies when comparing furniture pieces, such as two living room chairs that have exactly the same dimensions, but one is a carved wooden arm chair with only the seat upholstered and the other chair is entirely upholstered. The wooden chair appears to have less visual weight than the upholstered chair.

In order to create balance between the two chairs, if you wanted to use them on either side of a fireplace, you would need to place another object, such as a small table, covered with a floor-length tablecloth, beside the visually lighter weight chair, as shown in Figure 6. Another option is to add a throw and accent pillow to the lighter weight chair.

Figure 6

In addition to shape and mass, color and pattern also affect the visual weight of furniture:

- Bright, intense colors add visual weight
- Muted or neutral colors reduce visual weight
- Bold patterns add visual weight
- Solid colors or simple patterns reduce visual weight

Keep these factors in mind when arranging the furniture and accessories in your room. It isn't necessary to have perfectly symmetrical furniture arrangements on all your wall elevations, using identical objects on both sides of your composition, but try to keep the visual weight of your objects in balance.

Striving for balance, both in your furniture layout, as well as in your wall elevations will make your rooms feel more harmonious and inviting.

Mistake #6:
Moody Blues

Have you ever felt that being in a room had a negative effect on your mood, but you didn't know why? Three things that affect the mood of a room are: color, style of furnishings and lighting. Color is a very powerful decorating tool, and since the walls are the largest surface in any room, painting them is the least expensive but most dramatic change you can make. Color can completely transform the mood of any room, which affects the way you feel when you're in it.

You can use color to make a room feel bright or dark, cheerful or solemn, dramatic or casual, exciting or serene. Color can also create optical illusions to make small rooms seem more spacious or large rooms seem cozier. With the right color of paint, it's easy to camouflage a room's defects and highlight its positive features.

Even on a limited budget, appropriate use of color can bring a room to life. What mood do you want to create in your room? Choosing the right color scheme is simple once you make this decision.

When choosing a color scheme, you first need to decide whether you want to use cool or warm colors in your room. Cool colors are blue, green and violet. Warm colors are red, orange and yellow.

The natural light in the room can help you decide whether to choose warm or cool colors. If your room doesn't get any direct sunlight because it faces north, then the natural light in the room will be cool. Therefore, you might want to use warm colors in the room. If your room faces south and gets lots of sunlight, you might want to use cool colors.

Choose your color scheme according to the mood you want to create. Do you want to wake up to a warm and cheery yellow breakfast room? Do you prefer a cool, soothing and serene green for your bath? What about a dramatic, rich burgundy for a formal dining room?

Once you've decided on the color mood you want to use in the room, you're ready to select the specific colors for your color scheme. A color scheme can be built around one color or two or three colors.

When using more than one color, however, it's best to choose one of them as the predominant hue (the one you will paint on the walls), and use the other one or two colors as accents (for upholstery, window treatments and accessories). Try to distribute your accent colors evenly around the room to for balance.

You can create a color scheme from colors you like or from colors in the upholstered furniture you already own. You might also choose colors from an "inspiration piece", such as artwork, an area rug or a piece of fabric.

An easy way to choose your color scheme from an inspiration piece is to choose the lightest color in the artwork or fabric to paint the walls. Use one of the medium colors for a few of your solid-color upholstered furniture pieces and/or draperies. Pick one of the brightest colors for accents in the form of accessories, such as vases, throw pillows, frames, etc.

If you want to create a mood that represents a specific decorating style, such as French Country or Southwestern, then choose colors that are authentic to that particular style. It's easy to gather this type of information from the internet or books at your local library for whatever style you like.

When choosing colors for your walls, remember that dark colors make things seem smaller and closer. Therefore, dark colors can make a room seem smaller. Light colors make things seem larger and farther away, so light wall colors can make a room appear bigger.

To make a narrow room feel wider, paint the end walls a darker color, to make them appear to advance toward you, and use light colors on the long walls, to make them appear to recede into the distance.

After you've chosen the paint color for your walls, it's best to test it before painting the entire room. First, paint a full-size sheet of poster board and hang it on the wall. Observe how the color of the paint is affected by the natural light coming into the room at various times of the day. Also note how the artificial lighting in the room can change its appearance.

If you're satisfied with your paint test, then go ahead and paint your room. If not, you'll need to make another choice.

If you aren't comfortable with a bold color change on your walls, add color to your rooms gradually. Use accent pillows, throws, area rugs and accessories to add color. Next, try painting one wall as an accent, using a more vibrant or darker color. You can also add more color with window treatments.

If you want your color mood to be very warm or very cool, use an adjacent color scheme: two or three colors that are next to each other on the color wheel. For example: red and orange or blue, blue-green and green.

If you want the mood to be more neutral, use a complementary color scheme, two colors that lie directly opposite each other on the color wheel, such as red and green, blue and orange, or yellow and violet.

When deciding whether to use a light or dark wall color in your room, keep in mind that objects are more visible when placed against a sharply contrasting color background. Dark furniture placed against a light-colored wall will stand out more. If you want to camouflage an object (such as a piece of furniture that is too large for the space), place it in front of a similar colored background.

Don't ignore the power of color when decorating your home. Painting the walls is an inexpensive way to make a dramatic change. But choose your room's color scheme carefully, so it will have a positive effect on your mood and make the time you spend there more enjoyable.

Mistake #7: Floating Art & Other Mysteries

Accessorizing adds warmth and interest to any room. This is also an area where you can express your own unique style, using objects that you've collected over the years because they have special appeal. But it's important to use accessories that fit with the style of the décor you've chosen in order to create a more harmonious feel.

When choosing the accessories for your decorating project, pay careful attention to the mood each object projects. Does it match the style of your room? Do those silver, contemporary picture frames stick out like a sore thumb on your rustic country display shelf? With practice, you can train your eye to look for these details.

How many accessories should you use in your room? The style of your room's décor will help you decide how many to display. Some decorating styles, such as Victorian or English cottage, require many accessories to achieve their look, while a contemporary style uses very few.

Start by removing all the accessories in your room. Then try adding a few objects at a time; stopping occasionally to decide whether you have enough, too many or too few. Remember to consider the decorating style and mood you want to create—does it require more accessories or not as many.

Hanging Wall Art:

Wall art accessories include paintings, framed prints, tapestries, framed mirrors, wall screens and even some three dimensional objects such as sculptures, ornamental metalwork and sconces. Wall art is a very important part of the room's décor, therefore, it's important to display them properly.

One of the most common decorating mistakes is hanging artwork too high, so that it appears to be "floating" by itself on the wall. Hang wall art pieces low enough so they are viewed as part of a grouping of the furniture and other objects beneath them. When hanging a large piece of art over a sofa, it should be hung only about six to eight inches above the sofa back.

Wall art can help establish the focal point of a room. A focal point should dominate the eye from floor to ceiling in order to create the most impact, for example, a large framed mirror hung over a chest in a foyer or a painting hung over the fireplace mantel.

When hanging a large piece of wall art, make sure that its scale and shape are appropriate to the space where it will be hung. For example, the shape of the wall space above a sofa is usually a horizontal, rectangular shape. Therefore, the most appropriate shape for artwork to fit this space is a rectangular or oval shape, hung horizontally. If the wall space is square, use a square or round piece of artwork.

Next, observe the size of the art. Does it appear to be too large for the scale of the sofa, or is it too small to create the impact you want? If you don't have one piece of artwork that is large enough, use several smaller pieces in a grouping. Also, check to see that the color and style of the artwork, as well as the frame material, are compatible with the décor in your room.

Hang groups of pictures close enough together to present a cohesive unit, but not so close that they crowd each other. Make sure the overall dimensions of the grouping will fit the space you need to fill. Choose a similar frame material for all the pictures in the grouping—gold, silver, wood, lacquer, etc. The style of the frames should match that of the other furnishings, for example, rustic, contemporary, traditional, etc.

You can also mix pictures with other interesting shapes such as framed mirrors, shelves, sculptures, etc. in one grouping. When hanging groups of decorative objects on a wall, create your arrangement on paper first.

You can also trace the shapes of your frames or decorative objects onto brown paper, label them so you know which picture or object each one represents and cut them out. Use painter's tape to hang them on the wall. You can move them around until you get an arrangement you like, then hang the real wall art in place of each paper cutout.

Remember to balance the visual weight of the objects on either side of your imaginary center line when creating the wall art arrangement. Don't put all the large objects on one side and the small ones on the other.

Arranging Accessories in the Room:

The second category for accessories includes items such as vases, throw pillows, sculptures, plants, candelabras, framed photographs and clocks which are placed on the floor, tables, shelves or sofas and chairs.

When displaying small items, group similar objects together to create more of an impact (these might be objects made up of similar materials, such as silver or wood, or theme-related items, such as baskets, angels or vases).

Scattering small items around the room creates a cluttered feel, so group them together into collections. And remember, the smaller the items, the closer they need to be placed to the viewer. If you display a collection of small figurines on the top shelf of a tall bookcase, you won't be able to see them from such a distance.

Try not to overcrowd your displays. This also creates a cluttered feel, and the objects aren't being shown off to their best advantage.

Avoid covering every surface in your room with accessories. Remember that you or your guests might need a spot on an end table or coffee table to place a beverage. Your room isn't a museum for display purposes only; it also needs to function as livable space.

Using pairs of objects creates symmetry, which helps give the room a balanced look. Even with only three pieces in a display, a pair of things, such as candlesticks, flanking a large object, like a vase, will make a pleasing composition. Just remember, when displaying a group of accessories, you'll want the best visibility for all of the objects, so start by placing the tallest object in the back and arranging the rest in descending order of size.

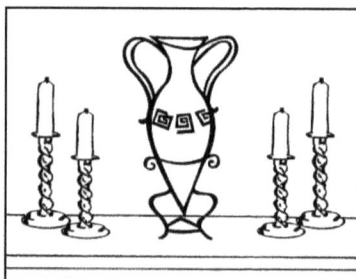

When decorating a bookcase, remember to use the "one-third" rule: one third books, one third accessories and one third open space. Don't overcrowd the shelves. You want to avoid a cluttered look.

When arranging a group of accessories on a table or shelf, use objects of varying heights, shapes, textures and sizes to create a more interesting display. Use attractive books or other objects to elevate some of the pieces to vary their heights.

When accessorizing, don't forget to address empty corners in your room. You can soften the sharpness of a corner by using accessories, such as a tall, potted plant or a smaller plant on a table, a tall statue or a smaller statue on a pedestal. You can use a tall floor lamp or smaller lamp on a table, a tall decorative folding screen or a lighted curio cabinet. There are many creative possibilities for adding interest to empty corners.

Think of every surface in your home as the basis for an artistic still life arrangement. Add decorative objects to the space above your cabinets in the kitchen or the top of an armoire in your bedroom. Don't overlook the floor as a potential surface for compositions. Place baskets or a collection of wooden boxes underneath end tables. Stack an assortment of fabric-covered boxes against a wall or at the end of a desk. Rest framed prints on the floor against a wall.

If you have a pleasing composition on one wall that you love to look at, place a mirror directly opposite the arrangement so you can enjoy the reflection as well.

Try to balance the soft and hard materials in a room. Too many hard surfaces make a room feel cold and uninviting. Use fabrics, greenery, rugs, tapestries and pillows to add softness and warmth.

Area rugs are accessories for the floor. They add color, texture and design patterns to your space. They can also help define a conversation area and cover cold, bare floors to make a room feel cozier. Adding an area rug is an easy and inexpensive way to change the look of a room. Rugs are sold at a variety of discount and home improvement stores in a wide range of prices.

Accessories add the finishing touch to any decorating project. Just keep in mind the number of accessories needed for the decorating style you've chosen, and try to use objects that fit with the mood, color and style of your room.

With a little practice and careful attention to detail, you'll be able to create a beautiful space that is an expression of your own personal style.

Designer Tip: The fireplace mantel is like a small stage, elevated above the rest of the room. Therefore, it's the perfect place to showcase your collectibles and establish a theme for your room. Gather your favorite collection, whether it's Victorian fans, African masks or Oriental vases and set the stage for your theme with an attractive mantle display.

Mistake #8:
A Shade Shy
and a
Valance Short

Window treatments dramatically affect the overall finished look of any room. There are hundreds of choices, including curtains, shades, blinds, shutters and valances. How do you decide which ones will work for your decorating project?

The most important thing to consider when choosing window treatments is the function they need to perform. Window coverings can provide privacy, block light, heat, cold or noise, as well as protect your furniture from the harsh rays of the sun. Make sure the window treatments you choose will perform the function you need.

Window coverings help soften the hard, rectangular lines of windows and enhance the décor of your room. You can use them to create a focal point if your room doesn't have an attractive architectural feature. They can also camouflage problems with the size and shape of your windows, which we'll discuss in the Designer Tricks section of this book.

A room's mood is determined by the colors, the style of furniture and accessories, and the lighting that is used in the space. The window treatments you choose should also complement the color and style of your décor.

For example, if your décor is contemporary, you wouldn't choose country style café curtains for your room. You also wouldn't use heavy velvet draperies in a casual breakfast room.

The fabric and hardware you choose will affect how formal or informal the window treatments will be. A swag made from tapestry fabric draped over an ornate metal pole is elegant and formal. But a swag made of cotton print fabric draped over a rustic wooden pole creates a more casual, informal look.

Another factor to keep in mind is that the window treatments should be suitable in scale with the size of the room. Heavy velvet draperies hung over a fussy Austrian shade, all hanging from a massive carved rod would be out of scale in a tiny sitting room with small scale furniture.

Below is a list of some of the choices for window coverings:

Blinds: Some of the many choices of blinds that are available include bamboo roll-up blinds or match-stick pull-up blinds which are more casual, create a tropical or Asian mood and can be used in a traditional or contemporary setting. Vertical blinds are typically used for informal, contemporary décor. Venetian blinds (horizontal slats) are more informal and are made from wood for a traditional setting or metal for a contemporary look.

Shades: Roman shades can be formal or informal, traditional or contemporary, depending on the fabric used. Austrian shades are formal and opulent. They are usually used in combination with draperies and valances in a traditional setting. Balloon shades (either pleated or gathered) are used in traditional décor, and can be formal or informal depending on the fabric chosen.

Shutters: Louvered wooden shutters are available in a variety of blade widths. The narrow blade shutters are more traditional and can be either formal or informal. Wide blade shutters work well for contemporary or tropical décor.

Draperies: Draperies (lined curtains) are made of heavier weight fabrics. They can be hung in a stationary position, called "dress draperies" or hung from hooks on traverse rods so they can be opened or closed, called "draw draperies". They can be used in combination with just about any of the other window treatments. Draperies can be formal or informal, traditional or contemporary, depending on the fabric used and how they are combined with other window treatments.

Curtains: Curtains are unlined panels of fabric, either sheer or opaque, that can be pleated, gathered onto rods through rod pockets or hung from rings or tabs. They have a lighter, more casual feel than draperies. Café curtains are hung from rings and cover only the bottom part of the window for a casual look.

Valances: Valances can be made of fabric or wood (cornice) and can be formal or informal depending on their fabric and shape, as well as how they are combined with other treatments.

Remember to keep the elements of function, style and scale in mind when planning for your window treatments.

When choosing design motifs for curtain fabrics, upholstery fabrics, wall paper and floor coverings, it's best to use only one bold pattern in the room. Good choices for secondary prints would be smaller scale stripes, dots, checks and plaids that coordinate with your color scheme and style of décor.

Another way to create harmony in your room is by repeating a color or pattern several times throughout the space. You can do this by using the same fabric from your window treatments in accent pillows for your sofa or chairs, or in a tablecloth on a side table.

Window coverings don't have to be expensive. There are many creative options for no-sew curtains, using lengths of fabric or flat sheets to drape across the tops of your windows in the form of swags as shown on page 35. You can also hang kitchen towels or lace panels from clip-on rings, or fabric napkins on the diagonal for a valance, as shown at right.

There are also a wide variety of inexpensive, ready-made curtain panels, valances and window shades available at discount stores and home improvement stores.

The possibilities for window treatments are unlimited. They can, however, be a substantial financial investment, whether you are making them yourself, buying them ready-made or having them custom made. But you can avoid costly mistakes if you remember to consider the function you need them to perform, as well as the style and scale of the room you're decorating.

Don't forget to re-design your window treatments when you re-design your room. They can make a dramatic change in the finished look.

Mistake #9: Shedding a Little Light

Ineffective lighting is another common decorating problem that can affect the function of a room and make it feel uninviting. Proper lighting is not only functional, it can dramatically affect the room's overall appeal.

Plan the lighting for your room the same way you planned all the other aspects of your design, by considering the function the lighting needs to perform and the mood you want it to create. Also check to see that your lighting is balanced throughout the space.

Function:

When planning for lighting, be sure to provide adequate light for the tasks you'll be performing in your room, such as reading, deskwork or hobbies that require good visibility, like sewing or crafting. Table lamps, floor lamps and wall-mounted swing-arm lamps are good choices for task lighting.

There should also be enough general (or ambient) lighting in the room to prevent it from being too dark. Use fixtures such as chandeliers, torchieres (floor lamps that shine light upward), sconces, recessed down lights and track lights for general lighting. It's a good idea to have a dimmer switch on these fixtures so you can vary the level of light in the room.

Mood:

There are three ways you can use lighting to influence the mood of a room: by the general feeling of the illumination (how bright or dim the lighting is), by the style of the light fixtures and by the use of accent lights.

The general illumination has the greatest effect on the room's mood. A brightly lit room projects a more work oriented mood, such as the light needed in a kitchen. A dimly lit room is more intimate and romantic, such as the level of light desirable in a bedroom. Decide what mood you want to create in your space in order to choose the type of lighting that will work best for your needs.

The light fixtures that you select express a certain style or mood. Some fixtures, such as table lamps, chandeliers and sconces, are more traditional and some are more contemporary in style. Some are lavish and ornate; others are simple and stark. As with the furniture you selected, lighting fixtures should complement the mood and style of your décor. For example, a modern chandelier would not be suitable in mood or style for a Victorian dining room.

You can provide accents of light in specific areas of a room to add a dramatic touch. This type of lighting is called accent lighting. A few examples are listed below:

- Use a floor can to shine light up through the foliage of a large plant

- Showcase a piece of art using a picture light or wall-washer (either ceiling mounted or portable floor light that shines light onto the walls)

- Use low-voltage rope lights (tiny lights inside a flexible plastic tube) on top of kitchen wall cabinets to provide indirect lighting

- Use a lamp on a table to brighten a dark corner

- Use rope lights inside shelving units or curio cabinets to highlight collectibles

- Use rope lights behind each curtain valance to provide a pleasant glow at night and highlight the fabric of the draperies in your room

Accent lighting not only highlights special artwork and brightens dark corners, it adds drama and interest to your overall design.

Lighting Fixture Choices:

The different lighting elements in a room need to work together to provide the right amount of light needed to perform specific tasks, as well as to achieve the overall mood you want in the room. Consider the following when planning for the lighting in your space:

- Add variety to your lighting plan. Use different types of lighting fixtures for different tasks. Some of the many options available include: table lamps, sconces, chandeliers, floor lamps, recessed down lights, wall washers (either ceiling mounted or portable floor can lights that shine light onto the walls), indirect lighting, low voltage rope lights and floor cans. Check out the many options available at your local home improvement store.

- Have the illumination in your room flow in different directions. Some fixtures project light upward (a torchiere or floor can light), some downward (ceiling mounted or recessed can lights in the ceiling) and some project light in all directions (a chandelier or table lamp with a translucent shade).

- Position lighting fixtures at different heights, from ceiling to floor—some at the ceiling, some on tables and some on the floor. Try to distribute them evenly around the room to create a more balanced feel.

- Plan for different levels of illumination in different parts of the room. Some areas should be bright (for reading), some less bright (for watching television). Use dimmer switches on general lighting, as well as task lighting to control the amount of light you want at different times.

Lighting is an important element when decorating your space. Be sure to give it the time and attention it deserves.

Take the time to create a lighting plan for your room. Proper lighting can dramatically affect the function, mood and beauty of any space. Make your rooms sparkle with the magic of lighting.

Mistake #10: Conflict or Harmony

Whatever style of furnishings and color scheme you choose, your goal is to create harmony in your living spaces. This means that all the décor in the room (the furniture, accessories, window treatments and floor and wall coverings) should harmonize with the mood you have chosen for the room. Striving for harmony in your design will help create that "pulled together" look you see in professionally decorated spaces.

Selecting Furniture Styles:

The style of furniture you select will determine the mood of your space. Do you want the room to be casual or formal, modern or traditional, masculine or feminine? If you're planning to use pieces you already own, then you'll need to plan your mood around those pieces.

If you want a contemporary mood for your room, and all the furniture you own is a rustic country style, then you'll either need to select a different mood to better accommodate your existing furniture, alter the look of your furniture with paint or upholstery, or purchase furniture that is more suitable for the mood you want to create in order to achieve a more harmonious feel for your space.

If the wooden furniture pieces you want to use are similar but different styles and the wood tones don't match, try to unify them by painting them and changing the hardware to match.

Tips for Painting Wooden Furniture:

- Wash the surface to remove any dirt or grease using a damp (not soaking) cloth and a mild solution of water and detergent. Let dry.
- Sand the surface lightly with fine grit sandpaper and remove any dust with a damp paper towel.
- Apply a coat of primer, using a paint brush or sponge roller. Check with your local paint store for the appropriate primer to cover the current finish, whether it is oil-based paint, water-based paint, stain, shellac, etc. Let the primer coat dry.
- Lightly sand the surface again and remove any dust.
- Ask the expert at your local paint store which type of paint is best for your project (oil-based or water-based). Apply your paint with a paint brush or sponge roller or use cans of spray paint and let dry. Add a second coat of paint if needed.

If you want to use mismatched upholstered furniture pieces that are fairly similar in style, cover them with matching or coordinating furniture slipcovers. There are many affordable choices for slipcovers available at discount stores, as well as on the Internet.

These covers also come in handy if you like to change the style of your room seasonally, from a heavier, winter feel to a lighter, summer look.

Scale:

Another important aspect to consider when selecting the furniture for your room is scale. Scale refers to the size of a piece of furniture in relation to the size of the other furniture in the room, or in relation to the size of the room itself. For example, a giant sofa in a tiny room is out of scale with the room. Large dining chairs crowded around a small dining table are out of scale with the table.

The easiest way to keep all the furniture in your room in scale is to start by choosing the most important piece first, such as the sofa for a living room or the dining table for a dining room. If you make sure that this piece is in scale with the room, and check carefully that all the other pieces of furniture are in scale with this piece, then you will have harmony in scale for the entire room.

After choosing the mood for your room, select pieces of furniture that fit with the style of your décor and are in scale with the size of your room in order to achieve a harmonious design.

Choosing Accessories:

The accessories you choose for your decorating project will also affect the mood of the room. As with the furniture selection, be sure your accessories fit with the style of your décor. For example, you wouldn't want to hang a stuffed deer head on the wall in your traditional, feminine bedroom, or display a delicate porcelain figurine on a rustic stone fireplace mantel.

Also remember that some decorating styles call for more accessories, such as country or cottage, and others require fewer, such as contemporary. Include only the number of accessories that you feel are appropriate for the decorating style you have chosen.

Another way to create harmony and continuity in your decorating scheme is to repeat a color or pattern at least three times in the room. Whether it is a type of metal finish, a fabric print, or a geometric shape, try to repeat it several times throughout the space. If the hardware on your cabinetry is bronze, repeat that finish in the lamp bases and picture frames. Use the same fabric from your window treatments in accent pillows on your chairs or a tablecloth on a side table.

Try to choose accessories that work with the mood of the room and are in harmony with the color and style of the décor. Pay close attention to the mood each object projects. Does it match the style of your room? With practice, you can train your eye to look for these details.

Choosing a Harmonious Color Scheme:

The colors you use on the walls, as well as for accents, should also be appropriate for the decorating style in your room. For example, sunny yellow, bright red and cobalt blue would be good choices for a French Country style, but not for an English Cottage style, which calls for soft pinks and greens.

If you're not sure what colors are suitable for the decorating style you've chosen, do some research at the library or on the Internet. The results will be well worth your effort.

The use of color is a very powerful decorating tool, which can affect the way you feel when you are in the room. If you want a soothing mood for a bedroom or bath, don't paint the walls an energizing color like orange. The warm colors: reds, yellows and oranges are more energizing. The cool colors: blues, greens and violets are more calming, especially the pastel versions. Neutral colors, such as beige and taupe are also more soothing. Paint the walls of your room a color that will evoke the mood you want.

When deciding on a color scheme, choose colors that are harmonious with the style of the décor you've chosen, as well as the mood you want to create.

Using Appropriate Lighting:

The lighting used in your space should also be appropriate for the mood you have chosen. Not only should the style of the light fixtures be harmonious with the rest of the décor, but the amount of light they produce should create the desired mood.

The lighting for a bedroom should be softer and more subtle than the bright lights required in a work space, such as a kitchen or craft room. The lighting in a dining room should be variable (on a dimmer switch) to change the mood from mid-morning brunch to elegant evening dinner party.

And don't forget to add accent lighting to brighten any dark corners in your space or highlight special artwork. These creative touches add an extra sparkle that can bring your room to life.

The Joy of Harmony:

In order to achieve harmony in your space, all the elements you choose for your room: the furniture, color scheme, window treatments, accessories and lighting, should work together to create the overall mood and style you envisioned.

If you pay close attention to the details of your design and practice your observation skills, you will sense when a particular object and its scale, style and color are not harmonious with the rest of your décor.

Your decorating goal should be to create a space that functions well for you and your family and adds beauty and joy to your life.

Don't worry about decorating trends and fads. Use the colors, furniture styles and accessories that you love. But pay attention to the details to make sure that all the elements in your room are working together to create a harmonious space.

Designer Tricks

There are many design "tricks of the trade" that you can use to create optical illusions to make your room appear different than it actually is. Whether you want to change the size or shape of your room or windows, or want to double an image, or make an object disappear, follow the guidelines below to help camouflage the negative features and highlight the positive features in your room.

Changing Room Dimensions

If you aren't happy with the dimensions or architectural features of your room, there are several designer tricks you can use to change its appearance through optical illusions.

Does the room feel too small or too narrow? Does the ceiling feel too low? Knowing how to choose the right wall treatments, furniture, window coverings and flooring can make all the difference. Choose the options below that best fit your room's needs:

To make a small room feel larger:

- Use small-scale furniture.

- Use solid color upholstery fabrics or fabrics with small design motifs.

- Avoid crowding the room with too much furniture.

- Paint the walls a light color to make them appear to recede. Paint doors and trim the same color as the walls to unify the space.

- The window treatment color should blend with the wall color, not contrast with it. Use either a solid color or small print for the fabric. If the curtains are made of print fabric, match the background color to the walls.

- Use small scale window treatments.

- Don't break up the floor space with area rugs.

To make a large room feel smaller:

- Select large-scale furniture and use plenty of pieces to keep the room from feeling empty.

- Light colored upholstery will make furniture appear bigger and fill the space better. Bright colors and bold design motifs also make furniture seem larger.

- Paint the walls a darker color and try to break up the space by painting wall moldings, baseboards and trim around doors and windows in a contrasting color.

- Use a different wall treatment on one or more of the walls, such as a painted accent wall, a wall mural or wallpaper.

- Use big and/or elaborate window treatments. Dark window treatments, like dark wall paint, will make the room appear smaller, but light window treatments will contrast with the darker walls to break up the space. Either choice is fine.

- Break up the floor space with area rugs. Large, bold design motifs for area rugs are fine as long as they don't compete with a different bold design pattern on the walls or furniture.

To make a narrow room feel wider:

- Paint the end walls a darker color to make them appear to "advance" and use light colors on the long walls to make them appear to "recede".

- Use a striped rug with the stripes running across the width.

- Cover one of the long walls with floor-to-ceiling mirrors.

- In a long, narrow hallway, avoid hanging art on the side walls. Instead hang a painting or framed print at the far end.

To make a low ceiling appear higher:

- Accentuate the vertical lines in the room by removing any horizontal moldings or paint them the same color as the walls.
- If using wallpaper, apply vertical patterns from floor to ceiling.
- Window treatments should also continue from floor to ceiling to avoid cutting the vertical height.
- Paint the ceiling a light color (white is best) to make it appear to recede.
- Darker colors on the floors make them appear to be lower than they actually are.

To make a high ceiling seem lower:

- Accentuate the horizontal lines on the walls by painting the horizontal trim (crown molding, chair rail and baseboards) in a contrasting color.
- Use contrasting wallpaper prints and/or paint colors above and below the chair rail, dividing the walls into two horizontal planes. If you don't have a chair rail, use a wallpaper border to divide the two treatments.
- Paint the crown molding the same color as the ceiling, or use a wallpaper border, matching the background color of the border to the ceiling color.
- Paint the ceiling a darker color than the walls.
- Lighter colors on the floors make them appear to be higher than they actually are.

Changing Window Dimensions with Curtains

Make a short window appear taller by adding a valance above it, starting the bottom edge of the valance just below the top edge of the window, and the top of the valance extends onto the wall space above the window.

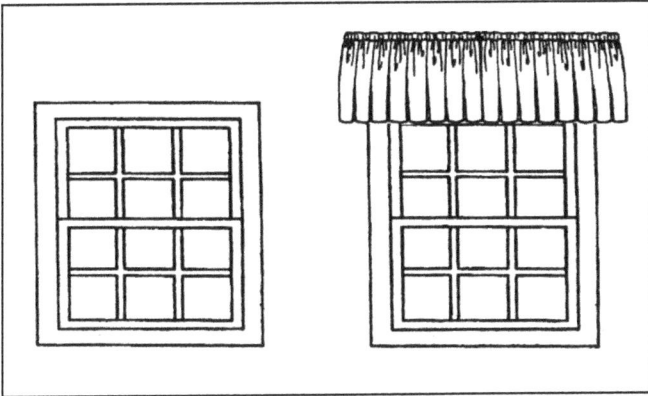

Make a tall window appear shorter by adding a valance, which starts near the top edge of the window and drops down to cover the top part of the window.

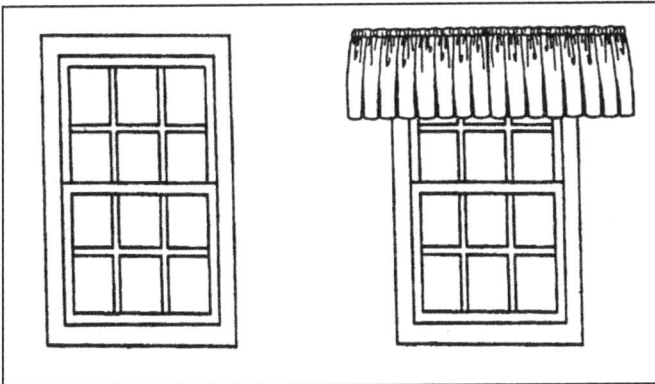

Make a wide window appear narrower by adding curtain panels to each side, starting close to the outside edge of the window and extending inside to cover some of its width.

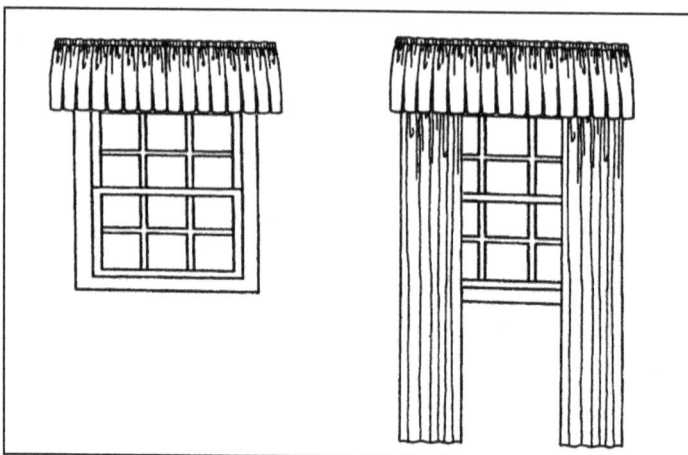

Make a narrow window appear wider by adding curtain panels to each side of the window, which start at the side edges of the window and extend beyond the outer edges of the window onto the wall.

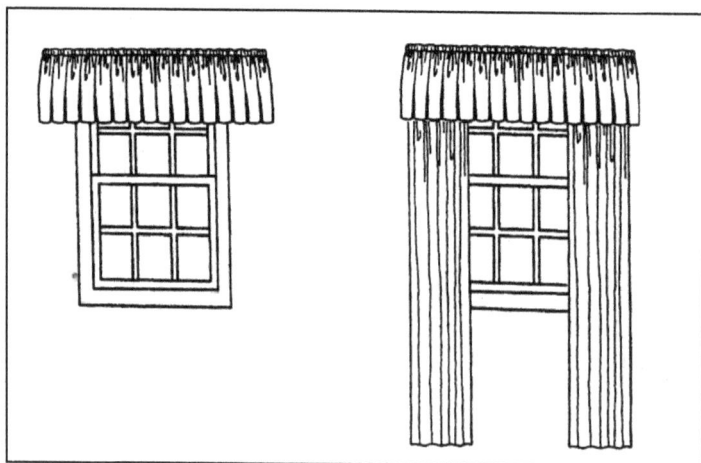

Adjust the heights of different size windows on the same wall by adding a valance that extends across the tops of both windows to make them appear the same height. Adjust their widths by adding curtain panels to each side to make them appear the same.

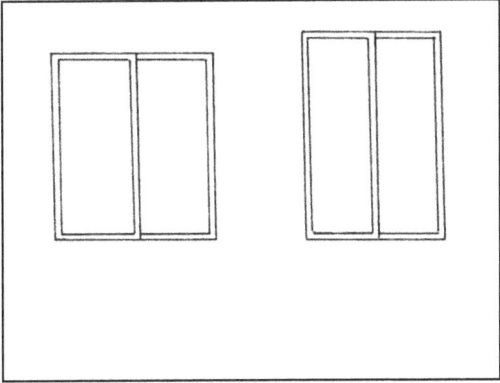

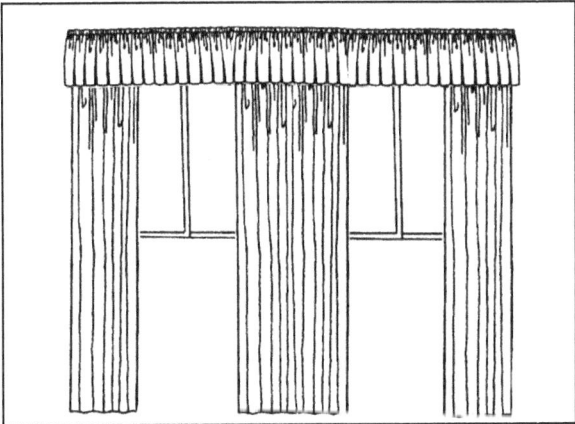

Designer Tricks
Using Mirrors

The unique characteristics of mirrors make them a very creative and useful decorating tool. Their reflective surfaces can increase the amount of light in your room, create optical illusions to make the space appear larger, or double the impact of any object they reflect.

Everyone knows that using wall-to-wall mirrors can make a room appear larger. Use any of the following techniques to achieve the results you want:

- In a narrow foyer, mirror an entire wall, which appears to double the size of the space.

- For very small spaces, such as a dining alcove, use mirrors on two walls that face each other. This produces the effect of infinite space because one wall reflects the other.

- If you want a soaring, two-story ceiling in your entryway, but yours is only eight feet high, cover the ceiling with mirrors to achieve the look of more height. (These mirrors should be installed by professionals.)

Decoratively framed mirrors can add a touch of elegance and style to any room, as well as being functional. A large framed mirror hung above a chest in a foyer, or over the fireplace mantel, can be the centerpiece of a focal point.

A tall, full-length, framed mirror looks great when leaned against a wall. Just make sure it's anchored to the wall for safety reasons. Hang a group of small, framed mirrors together on a wall to create architectural interest.

Windowpane mirrors (a piece of wall art that looks like a window with a mirror behind it) can create the illusion of a real window on a blank wall. They come in a wide variety of shapes, sizes and decorating styles, and work great with any décor.

If your desk faces a wall without a window, hang a mirror on the wall in front of you that will reflect a more pleasing view behind you, such as a piece of artwork or a window with a view.

Another creative use for mirrors is to install them as a backsplash behind a stove. Not only are they easy to clean, but they reflect light into the work area and act as a rear-view mirror so you can see what's going on behind you. These can also be used as backsplashes over kitchen countertops, creating the same effect.

You can double the impact of your artwork or windows by placing mirrors opposite them to repeat the image from another angle in the room. Whenever you hang a mirror in a room, always check to make sure that it is reflecting a pleasant image.

In addition to being attractive accessories, mirrors are also functional. Hanging a mirror in the foyer makes it easy to check your appearance before leaving. Just be sure to hang it at an appropriate height for viewing.

Mirrors can also be used to make objects "disappear". If you have an unsightly post standing in the middle of your room, which cannot be removed because it is structurally necessary, cover it with mirrors. They will reflect the objects in the room, making the post less noticeable. The same trick works for an over-scaled, square or rectangular coffee table or dining room table.

The Power of Illusions

When used effectively, these designer tricks can dramatically change the appearance of a room's scale or proportions to camouflage negative architectural features or accentuate positive features. Which negative features in your room do you want to change? Which ones do you want to highlight? Now that you know how to use these designer tricks, you'll be able to make your rooms look their best.

Interior Re-Design

By using the decorating tips and suggestions described in this book, you can re-design the interior spaces of your home, using the furniture and accessories you already own to make your rooms more functional and beautiful.

Follow the steps listed below to complete your re-design project:

1. Start with a clean slate by removing everything from the room, if possible.

2. This is a good time to decide if you want to paint the room, or perhaps just paint an accent wall.

3. Decide on the function of your room and scour your entire house to find the furniture pieces you'll need. A furniture re-design is based on the assumption that your furniture is in good condition. If your furniture is extremely worn or dirty, or if you hate the color or style, you might consider getting slipcovers for the upholstered pieces and refinishing or painting the wooden pieces.

4. Arrange the furniture in the room, following the decorating suggestions in this book for balance, traffic patterns, comfortable conversation areas and general layout.

5. Carefully consider the window treatments in your room. Will they work with your new décor? If not, try to find creative but inexpensive methods to make them harmonize with the color and style of your decorating scheme.

6. Add the appropriate lighting to make your room sparkle. You'll need general lighting to light the overall room, task lighting for specific areas, and accent lighting to brighten dark corners and highlight special artwork on walls or shelves. Check to see that the lighting is balanced throughout the space.

7. Accessorize your room using the suggestions listed previously in this book. Search your home for any accessories that would be suitable in style and color for your new space. Don't forget area rugs, pillows, throws, framed prints or mirrors, real or silk greenery and anything else you might find to create interesting displays that will add beauty to your room. Remember to distribute your accent colors evenly around the space and display all art pieces where they create the most impact.

Quick Change
Decorating

Are you tired of the same old décor, but either the budget or time restraints can't accommodate a major redo? Try a few of the following tips to give your rooms a quick change without spending a lot of money or time.

- Instead of painting the entire room, paint just an accent wall. Use a totally different color that coordinates with your existing furniture, perhaps something a bit more daring. You might try a bright, cheerful color in the kitchen or breakfast room, or maybe a darker, more dramatic color in the living room or dining room.

- Re-arrange the furniture in your room using the decorating guidelines presented in this book. You'll get a whole new look for zero dollars and very little time.

- If your upholstered furniture pieces are looking a bit worn or dated, cover them with slip covers. This is also an easy and inexpensive way to change the look of your room with the seasons, from a heavier winter look to a lighter summer feel.

- Add new window treatments. You can also change their look seasonally by removing heavier winter draperies and using a simple valance over sheer curtains or blinds.

- Change the throw pillows in your room. Whether you buy them, make your own, or add trims to store-bought pillows, they can help change the color and style of your room. You can change them out with each season or add holiday pillows for extra punch. Throw pillows can create a whole new look for very little cost.

- Draping a throw over a chair or sofa can add new color, texture and style to your room. It can also hide an unsightly stain or tear in the upholstery. During the winter, it provides a cozy touch that is also functional in case you feel a chill.

- Adding an area rug is another easy and inexpensive way to change the look of a room. Rugs are sold at a variety of discount and home improvement stores in a wide range of prices. They can add color and texture, help define a conversation area, make a room feel cozier, or completely change the room's style. Use darker, more vibrant colors in thick, plush carpets for a winter feel and lighter, airy colors in light-weight woven rugs for a summer look.

- Accessories and wall art are the finishing touches in any room. Moving these pieces from one room to another can create a quick decorating change. Collect similar items that you have scattered throughout your home and display them together in one room to create a new theme. For instance, gather your husband's sports memorabilia and arrange it in a home office or den.

- A new piece of wall art might be just the focal point your room needs. You can find inexpensive framed prints at many discount stores, furniture resale stores or garage sales. It might inspire you to take your room's décor in a whole new direction. Changing the accessories and wall décor is an easy way to give your room a quick makeover.

- Add inexpensive new accessories, such as candles to match your new color scheme or greenery (real or silk) to add softness and life to the space. Include flea market finds, such as baskets or ornamental metal pieces which can be painted to coordinate with your décor.

- Change out the lampshades in your room. You can purchase inexpensive shades at many home improvement or discount stores. Or spruce up a lampshade you found at a garage sale or one you already own by painting it, covering it with fabric or simply adding trims such as beading or braid. You can do the same thing with most lamp bases for a whole new look.

- Add accent lighting to create drama and brighten any dark corners. An inexpensive floor can placed behind a tall plant will create highlights and patterns on the walls and ceiling. Add a small picture light to emphasize a special piece of wall art. Place a string of low-voltage rope lights inside a curio cabinet to showcase collectibles. Refer to page 40 for more accent lighting suggestions. These are all quick, low-budget tricks that can add a bit of sparkle to any room.

Make your home an expression of your own personal style. Changing your décor doesn't have to cost a bundle. All it takes is a little time and effort and a lot of creativity.

Putting It All Together

Your home should be your sanctuary—a haven from the frantic pace of the world outside. We all want our living spaces to be functional, comfortable and beautiful.

Taking the time to create a plan for how your rooms need to function and providing the necessary furniture and lighting to meet your needs will make your home more enjoyable and relaxing.

Adding beauty to your living spaces with colors you love and furniture and accessories that you find appealing will have a positive affect on your mood and add joy to your life.

Use the guidelines and tips presented in this book to avoid some of the most common decorating mistakes and create a more comfortable and inviting home for yourself and your family.

Index

About the Author

Gloria Hander Lyons has channeled 30 years of training and hands-on experience in the areas of art, interior decorating, crafting and event planning into writing creative how-to books. Her books cover a wide range of topics including decorating your home, cooking, planning weddings and tea parties, crafting and self-publishing. She has designed original craft projects featured in magazines, such as *Better Homes and Gardens, McCall's, Country Handcrafts* and *Crafts*.

She teaches interior decorating, self-publishing and wedding planning classes at her local community college. Much to her family's delight, her kitchen is in non-stop test mode, creating recipes for new cookbooks.

Visit her website for free craft ideas, decorating and event planning tips and tasty recipes at: www.BlueSagePress.com.

Other Books by Gloria Hander Lyons

- *Easy Microwave Desserts in a Mug*
- *Easy Microwave Desserts in a Mug for Kids*
- *No Rules – Just Fun Decorating*
- *Just Fun Decorating for Tweens & Teens*
- *Decorating Basics: For Men Only!*
- *If Teapots Could Talk—Fun Ideas for Tea Parties*
- *The Super-Bride's Guide for Dodging Wedding Pitfalls*
- *Designs That Sell: How To Make Your Home Show Better and Sell Faster*
- *A Taste of Lavender: Delectable Treats with an Exotic Floral Flavor*
- *Lavender Sensations: Fragrant Herbs for Home & Bath*
- *Self-Publishing on a Budget: A Do-It-All-Yourself Guide*
- *Hand Over the Chocolate & No One Gets Hurt! The Chocolate-Lover's Cookbook*
- *The Secret Ingredient: Tasty Recipes with an Unusual Twist*
- *Flamingoes, Poodle Skirts & Red Hots: Creative Theme Party Ideas*

Ordering Information

To order additional copies of this book, send check or money order payable to:

Blue Sage Press
48 Borondo Pines
La Marque, TX 77568

Cost for this edition is $6.95 per book plus $3.00 shipping and handling for the first book and $1.50 for each additional book shipped to the same address (U.S. currency only).

Texas residents add 8.25% sales tax to total order amount.

To pay by credit card or get a complete list of books written by Gloria Hander Lyons, visit our website at:

www.BlueSagePress.com